T0011496

Animal and Plant Extinction

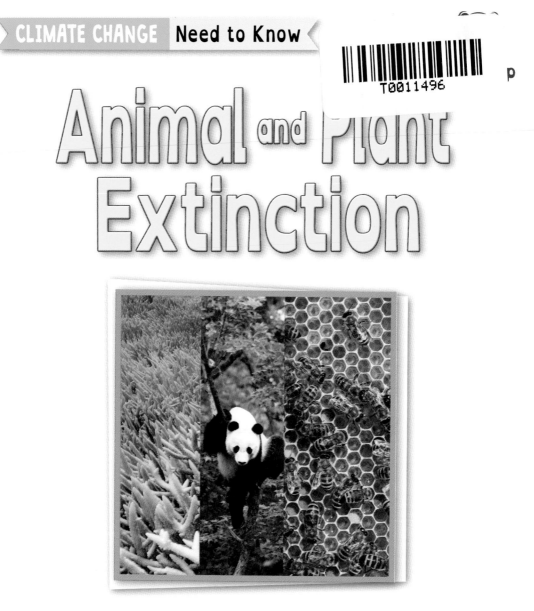

by Jane Parks Gardner

Consultant: Jordan Stoleru,
Science Educator

BEARPORT
PUBLISHING

Minneapolis, Minnesota

Credits

Cover and title page, © The physicist/Adobe Stock and © Rainer von Brandis/iStock and © saqib memon/iStock; 5, © Silfox/iStock; 7, © Warpaintcobra/iStock; 9T, © Lukasz Pawel Szczepanski/Shutterstock; 9B, © Jan Martin Will/Shutterstock; 11, © Jeffrey T. Kreulen/Shutterstock; 12–13, © givaga/Shutterstock; 15, © Bosku123/Shutterstock; 16, © Chartcharn Phodhiphad/Shutterstock; 17, © loeskieboom/iStock; 18, © Fernando M. Elkspera/Shutterstock; 19, © Vladimir Martinov/Shutterstock; 21, © Michael Potter11/Shutterstock; 23T, © bmf-foto.de/Shutterstock; 23B, © Chuck Wagner/Shutterstock; 24, © Robert Whyte / Greg Anderson/Creative Commons Attribution 2.0; 24–25, © Toa55/Shutterstock; 27, © Lotus_studio/Shutterstock; 28L, © Ian Bell, EHP, State of Queensland/Creative Commons Attribution 3.0 au; 28ML, © Sheep81/Public Domain; 28MR, © Charles H. Smith/U.S. Fish and Wildlife Service Public Domain; 28R, © Mike Weston/Creative Commons Attribution 2.0.

Bearport Publishing Company Product Development Team

President: Jen Jenson; Director of Product Development: Spencer Brinker; Managing Editor: Allison Juda; Associate Editor: Naomi Reich; Associate Editor: Tiana Tran; Art Director: Colin O'Dea; Designer: Elena Klinkner; Designer: Kayla Eggert; Product Development Assistant: Owen Hamlin

STATEMENT ON USAGE OF GENERATIVE ARTIFICIAL INTELLIGENCE
Bearport Publishing remains committed to publishing high-quality nonfiction books. Therefore, we restrict the use of generative AI to ensure accuracy of all text and visual components pertaining to a book's subject. See BearportPublishing.com for details.

Library of Congress Cataloging-in-Publication Data

Names: Gardner, Jane P., author.
Title: Animal and plant extinction / by Jane Parks Gardner ; consultant:
   Jordan Stoleru, Science Educator.
Description: Minneapolis, Minnesota : Bearport Publishing Company, [2024] |
   Series: Climate change: need to know | Includes bibliographical
   references and index.
Identifiers: LCCN 2023030954 (print) | LCCN 2023030955 (ebook) | ISBN
   9798889165231 (library binding) | ISBN 9798889165309 (paperback) | ISBN
   9798889165361 (ebook)
Subjects: LCSH: Extinction (Biology)–Juvenile literature. | Climatic
   changes–Juvenile literature.
Classification: LCC QH78 .G37 2024 (print) | LCC QH78 (ebook) | DDC
   576.8/4–dc23/eng/20230722
LC record available at https://lccn.loc.gov/2023030954
LC ebook record available at https://lccn.loc.gov/2023030955

For more information, write to Bearport Publishing, 5357 Penn Avenue South, Minneapolis, MN 55419.

Contents

Pity the Pika

A tiny pika scrambles up a mountain. Temperatures are on the rise, and the little animal can't take the heat. The furry critter might be on its way toward **extinction**, and it's not alone. Why are so many animals and plants at risk?

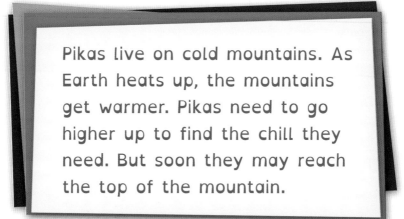

Pikas live on cold mountains. As Earth heats up, the mountains get warmer. Pikas need to go higher up to find the chill they need. But soon they may reach the top of the mountain.

A pika

What Is Extinction?

Extinction is the process of living things dying out completely. When a **species** of plant or animal is extinct, it is gone forever.

Dinosaurs went extinct. There used to be many kinds of bananas. Now, there are only a few kinds. The others are extinct.

Many plants and animals have lived on the planet over its long history. However, more than 90 percent of those species have gone extinct.

There are many reasons plants and animals become extinct. Sometimes, there are natural causes. Asteroids and volcanoes have killed off living things in the past.

Today, humans are causing a lot of harm. We are changing the planet with some of the actions we take every day.

There have been five **mass extinctions** in Earth's history. This means many species disappeared at the same times. Studies show we may be getting close to another mass extinction event!

Some think an asteroid killed the dinosaurs. Polar bears might be part of the next wave of extinction.

A Changing Climate

Life on Earth is facing **climate change.** Humans put gases into the air when we burn **fossil fuels** to power our homes, cars, and businesses. The gases trap heat around Earth. This warms the air, land, and water. It changes the climate of our planet.

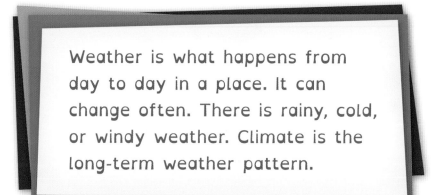

Weather is what happens from day to day in a place. It can change often. There is rainy, cold, or windy weather. Climate is the long-term weather pattern.

The more fossil fuels we burn, the more heat-trapping gases they make.

The average temperature in much of the world is getting hotter. The amount of **precipitation**, or rain and snow, has also been affected. Plants and animals are being forced to **adapt** to these changes. If they can't, they may go extinct.

Since 1880, Earth has warmed by about 2 degrees Fahrenheit (1 degree Celsius). It is predicted to warm another 2°F (1°C) by 2050 and an additional 3-7°F (2-4°C) by 2100.

Harming Homes

Some plants and animals can survive only when it is certain temperatures. As Earth's climate changes, they are at risk of overheating.

Worse yet, some **habitats** are disappearing in the heat. Ice around the Arctic and Antarctic is melting. The frozen homes of polar bears and penguins are shrinking away.

Polar bears hunt on sea ice. They also use the ice to rest after long swims. With less ice, there are fewer places to hunt. They have to swim further without taking breaks.

Cold, snowy habitats where arctic foxes live are heating up.

Melting ice also causes sea levels to rise. Plants and animals along the coast struggle when land that was once dry becomes soaked in salty water. Sometimes, whole islands are covered, along with the plants and animals that live there.

Freshwater turtles live along the coast. They need a mix of fresh and salt water to stay alive. However, salt levels can increase as the sea levels rise. Too much salt can kill them.

A Vanishing Feast

For animals that can beat the heat or escape rising water, finding food might be the next challenge. Other climate-related changes may push food sources out of a habitat. Heat may dry up water to drink.

Galapagos damselfish once lived throughout the Galapagos Islands. Then in the 1980s, the islands' waters got warmer. The plankton these fish ate died. Without their food, Galapagos damsels disappeared.

Life Connections

When a single species goes extinct, its whole habitat suffers. The plants and animals in a place often depend upon one another for their food and water. Top predators keep the populations of other creatures in check. And without certain plant life, some animals can't make their homes.

African elephants dig water holes. These sources of water become more important as African savannas become drier. When elephants leave habitats, other creatures that rely on them for water are put at risk.

Water holes are important for many animals in the savanna.

Extreme Events

Climate change is causing more frequent and more extreme **severe weather.** Warmer ocean waters feed stronger hurricanes. These storms can kill a lot of things at once. Hurricanes Maria and Irma wiped out many of the few remaining Puerto Rican parrots. Hurricane Irma also killed many Florida Key deer.

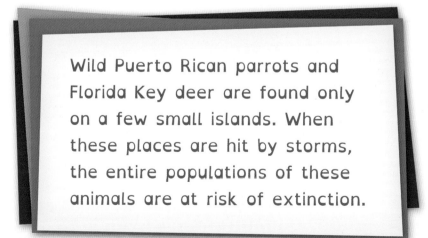

Wild Puerto Rican parrots and Florida Key deer are found only on a few small islands. When these places are hit by storms, the entire populations of these animals are at risk of extinction.

Puerto Rican parrot

Florida Key deer

Hot, dry weather has become more common due to climate change. This increases the risk of droughts. Plants are drying out and dying without rain. With just one spark, a wildfire can light up a dry habitat. As fires rage, they can kill many plants and animals.

Wildfires burned Australian forests from late 2019 into early 2020. The fires killed more than 10 percent of the koalas on the continent. For a time, scientists believed assassin spiders became extinct due to the wildfires.

What Can We Do?

Fortunately, we are always learning more about climate change. Scientists are working to protect plants and animals in the changing world. Many people are trying to reduce the use of fossil fuels. This will slow climate change. And it may be just enough to stop some plants and animals from going extinct.

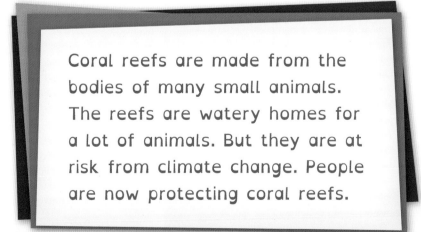

Coral reefs are made from the bodies of many small animals. The reefs are watery homes for a lot of animals. But they are at risk from climate change. People are now protecting coral reefs.

Animals on the Edge

More and more animals are at risk of going extinct as the climate continues to change. In the last 15 years alone, the number has doubled.

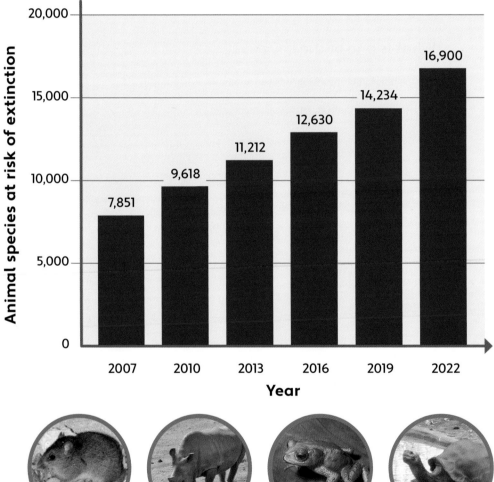

Animal species at risk of extinction vs. Year

Year	Animal species at risk of extinction
2007	7,851
2010	9,618
2013	11,212
2016	12,630
2019	14,234
2022	16,900

Bramble Cay melomy

Northern white rhino

Golden toad

Pinta Island tortoise

★ SilverTips for REVIEW

Review what you've learned. Use the text to help you.

Define key terms

adapt   extinction
climate   weather
climate change

Check for understanding

What is one of the key causes of climate change?

What is extinction, and how has it changed over time?

Name two ways climate change harms animals and plants.

Think deeper

How would fewer changes to the climate impact the future for global plant and animal life? What is one way to make this happen?

★ SilverTips on TEST-TAKING

- **Make a study plan.** Ask your teacher what the test is going to cover. Then, set aside time to study a little bit every day.

- **Read all the questions carefully.** Be sure you know what is being asked.

- **Skip any questions** you don't know how to answer right away. Mark them and come back later if you have time.

Glossary

adapt to change over time to survive in an environment or habitat

climate change changes in the usual weather patterns around Earth, including the warming of the air and oceans, due to human activities

extinction when a type of animal or plant dies out

fossil fuels fuels such as coal, oil, and gas made from the remains of plants and animals that died millions of years ago

habitats the places in nature where plants and animals live

mass extinctions events during which many living things go extinct within a short period of time

precipitation water in the form of rain, snow, sleet, or hail

severe weather dangerous weather events that can cause damage or loss of life

species groups that animals are divided into, according to similar characteristics

Read More

Bergin, Raymond. *Animals in Danger (What on Earth? Climate Change Explained).* Minneapolis: Bearport Publishing Company, 2022.

Faust, Daniel R. *Global Warming (Climate Change: Need to Know).* Minneapolis: Bearport Publishing Company, 2024.

Taylor, Barbara. *The Magnificent Book of Extinct Animals.* San Rafael, CA: Weldon Owen Children's Books, 2021.

Learn More Online

1. Go to **www.factsurfer.com** or scan the QR code below.

2. Enter "**Animal Plant Extinction**" into the search box.

3. Click on the cover of this book to see a list of websites.

Index

About the Author

Jane Parks Gardner has written more than 60 books. Her favorite topics to write about include plate tectonics, climate change, and marine animals (especially octopuses)!